MICHELLE P.

JEAN

MELANIA

MADGE

FLORETTA

BARBARA

PHILOMENA

YVETTE

NADYA

JOANNE

BRITTANY

GLORIA

ANASTASIA

ONDINE

SHARON

KATHLEEN

KIMBRE

CECILLE

LORRAINE

VERA

WILLA

Feathered & FABULOUS

This isn't "Lifestyles of the Adequately Compensated."

Feathered
& FABULOUS

Wit and Wisdom from Glamorous Birds

By Alison Throckmorton

CHRONICLE BOOKS
SAN FRANCISCO

Parenting routinely pushed the limits of Helen's medication.

Husbands may come
and go, but alimony
is forever.

My advice?
Spend your money
now while you can.
It's a coffin,
not a condo.

Behind every happy woman is a trail of fragile male egos.

My favorite
meal is vodka.

Theresa's bedroom is busier than a bus station.

Vanessa's blood alcohol content is higher than her IQ.

My future is marriage
or murder.

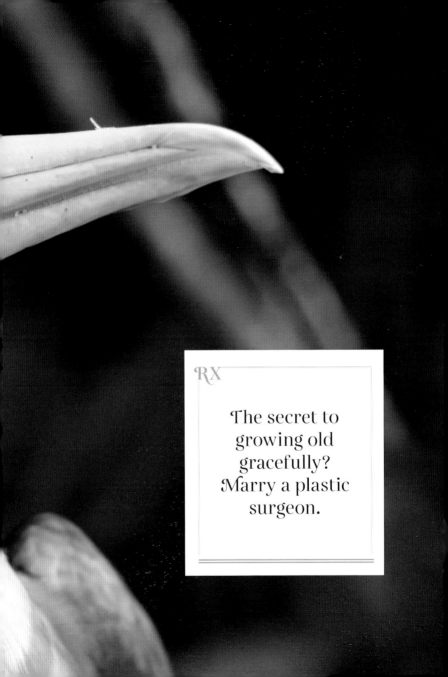

RX

The secret to
growing old
gracefully?
Marry a plastic
surgeon.

It's all fun and games until you're single, childless, independently wealthy . . . wait, never mind. It's still fun and games.

At this point, Maeve was held together by shapewear, pills, and rage.

Her legs were her best asset, and Patrice wasn't afraid to show them off.

Elaine hated golf, so she spent most of the time at the clubhouse, drinking too many bellinis and gossiping with the other wives.

Bernadette knew the haircut was edgy, but she didn't expect to get hit on by *both* baristas, who were obviously in their 20s.

Barbara
hasn't had
sex in six
years . . .

After husband number three
left with her dignity and most
of her money, Justine found it
hard to keep giving a damn.

Much to her family's
dismay, Sheila decided
it was time to shed the
stereotypes of her age and
go to Burning Man.

Felice worried that
she had taken the
"New Year, New You"
concept too far.

Despite her ex-husband's *exhaustive* stupidity, Marion refused to get into a battle of wits with an unarmed opponent.

Lilian always looked
her best, despite always
being hungover.

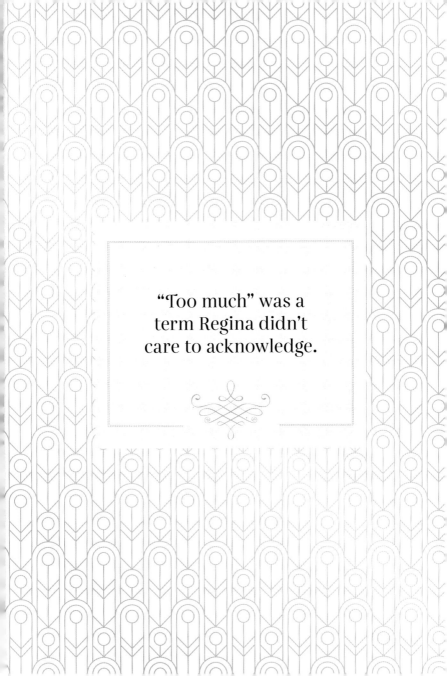

"Too much" was a
term Regina didn't
care to acknowledge.

Despite raving from the other women, Lucille had never heard of Costco and never plans to visit.

Caroline felt a thrill knowing that soon she wouldn't have to listen to Gregory's bullshit anymore.

Though Imogen believed in love, she also believed in a stiff drink and a CPA who knows when to keep his mouth shut.

Alison Throckmorton is a writer, editor, and mother of two living in the San Francisco Bay Area. Much like the birds she writes about, she's very fancy. Unlike the birds she writes about, she channels her rage into more meaningful pursuits, like snarky embroidery and tending her chickens.

Farrah knew that a nude oil painting of herself was just what she deserved.

Deep down Vera knew . . .
she should have bought
a fourth bottle of wine.

Beatrice refused
to dine alone, so
she brought her
emotional baggage
along with her.

Esme knew
that revenge is a
dish best served
cold. Until then,
however, a frozen
margarita would
have to do.

Joanna listened with
growing exasperation
as Frederick explained
exactly how she
should feel.

I'm on a diet
of alcohol
and vitriol.

Library of Congress Cataloging-in-Publication Data available.

ISBN 978-1-7972-0458-1

Manufactured in China.

Text by Alison Throckmorton.
Design by Michael Morris.

10 9 8 7 6 5 4 3 2 1

Chronicle Books LLC
680 Second Street
San Francisco, CA 94107
www.chroniclebooks.com

ANASTASIA

ONDINE

SHARON

KIMBRE

KATHLEEN

CECILLE

LORRAINE

VERA

WILLA

ADELAIDE

NOREEN

MARIEL

STEFANIE

TONYA

BATHSHEBA

DARLENE

ALEXANDRA

JOSEPHINE

DIANE

MICHELLE C.